The Tao of
Supply Chain Management

*160 serious and not-so-serious
random rules and tips for the
supply chain manager*

Clifford F. Lynch
www.cflynch.com

Cover by Lamar Caldwell
Layout by Cheryl McMains
ISBN 0-9744167-3-8

Copyright 2006 CFL Publishing
P.O. Box 770398
Memphis, TN 38177-0398
E-mail: cliff@cflynch.com Website: www.cflynch.com

Printed in the United States of America. by Instantpublisher.com
No parts of this book may be reproduced in any form or
by any means without permission from the Publisher.

About the Title

The *Tao Te Ching*, written over 2,500 years ago, presented in 81 short chapters a treatise on life and how it should be lived. There was no apparent organization to it; rather it was a randomly compiled user's manual for Taoism.

This handbook, while not as old, is organized no better.

Thirty spokes converge upon a single hub; it is on the hole in the center that the use of the cart hinges.

- Tao Te Ching, *Chapter 11*

The Tao of Supply Chain Management

The Tao of Supply Chain Management

INTRODUCTION

Supply chain management has become one of the most important areas of concentration for firms around the globe. Because of its broad scope, many logistics managers are rushing to educate themselves in new disciplines, while others are keeping their heads down, hoping for the best.

It is becoming clear to all, and painful to some, that the successful supply chain executive will be the one who has mastered the arts of collaboration, cooperation, and relationships. To manage such an all-inclusive function efficiently will require the skills of negotiation and persuasion, and most of all, sensitivity to others both inside and outside the firm.

This book is intended to serve as a reminder of some basic facts of SCM, but more importantly, an admonition that business should be fun.

- Clifford F. Lynch
January, 2006

4 The Tao of Supply Chain Management

1.

Learn what the supply chain is...

2.

…Now learn to define it in 25 words or less.

3.

Practice saying CSCMP until you can do it flawlessly.

6 The Tao of Supply Chain Management

4.

Enhance your industry wisdom by learning what NCPDM stands for.

5.

Don't underestimate the power of corporate politics.

6.

Collaboration is the act of working jointly with others or together, especially in an intellectual endeavor.

7.

Collaborationism is the advocacy or practice of collaboration with an enemy.

The Tao of Supply Chain Management

8.

Don't get the two confused.

9.

Collaboration is the glue that holds the supply chain together.

10. Sometimes glue is scarce.

11.

In some firms, it doesn't exist.

12.

One good way of learning
collaboration is to return phone calls.

13.

A best practice is the one after which your piano teacher tells you that you just might make it in music.

14.

Think globally.

15. Act globally.

16.

If you don't know how, find someone to teach you.

14 The Tao of Supply Chain Management

17. $24/7 = 3.4$

18.

Machiavelli was not a supply chain manager.

19.   He very well could have been.

20.

Have your own agenda.

21.
Every other manager in the supply chain will have one.

22. Learn what they are.

23.

Use them to your advantage.

24.

A vertical is not necessarily the opposite of a horizontal.

25. Paradigm = 4 nickel

26.
Sales forecasts, like weather forecasts, are rarely correct...

27.
Metrics are the real measure of supply chain success.

28.
Don't keep them a secret from your employees.

29. Performance measurement should be balanced

30. Don't measure everything every day.

31.
Learn to manage before you try to measure.

32.
Core competency is what you do best.

33.
It is not meant to describe your proficiency with a Granny Smith apple.

34.
When trying to make a point to management, don't benchmark companies that are better at SCM than you are.

35. For every win-win, there is a win-lose.

36.

For every tenth win-win, there is a lose-lose.

37.
A lean supply chain is desirable.

38.
Learn how to define it.

39.
Learn to discuss it intelligently.

40.
Learn to implement it even more intelligently.

24 The Tao of Supply Chain Management

41.

Products should be *pulled* by customer demand, not *pushed* at the convenience of the manufacturing facility.

42. Do not minimize the human factor in implementing lean.

43. Do not ignore the cultural changes that will be required.

44.

Honor your commitments.

The Tao of Supply Chain Management

45. Good outsourcing relationships are mutually beneficial.

46. Bad ones are not.

47.
Logistics service providers are not the enemy.

48.

Beware of "cost-plus percentage" outsourcing contracts.

49.

Gain sharing is a good thing.

50.

Be sure there are gains to share.

51. Poor communication is second only to poor planning as a cause of outsourcing relationship failure.

52. If all else fails, read the contract.

53.

LSP's should establish pricing based on their own costs, not their competitors'.

54.
For an outsourcing relationship to succeed, it must be based on a keen sense of mutual trust and respect.

55.

A contract that yields no profit will yield no satisfaction.

56. Every change you make to your supply chain should add value.

57.
Everything you are doing now should add value.

58. If it isn't, get rid of it.

59.

As a rough rule of thumb, inventory is proportionate to the square root of the number of warehouses.

60.
Managing transportation is not as much fun as it used to be.

61.

Transportation Management Systems have become the definitive tools in managing transportation costs more effectively.

The Tao of Supply Chain Management

62. Learn to find China on the map.

63. It is shaped a little like a pelvis and is just south of Mongolia.

34 The Tao of Supply Chain Management

64.

NASCAR drivers are results-driven.

65.
So should the supply chain manager be.

The Tao of Supply Chain Management

66.

Managing an entire supply chain is not easy.

67. Some experts distinguish supply chain and logistics management.

68. Others consider the terms to be interchangeable.

69.
The first group are real experts.

70. The others are not.

71.
A good logistician is not necessarily a good supply chain manager.

72.
A good supply chain manager is not necessarily a good logistician.

73.
In making acquisitions, beware of the "greater fool" selling philosophy.

74.
Being the greater fool is not a good thing.

75.
EBITDA is not necessarily a good measurement of financial performance.

76.
It can be if the tooth fairy provides all the capital expenditures.

77.
Supply chain management is relationship-driven — not operationally-driven.

78. If yours isn't, you're probably in for trouble.

79.
Relationships require a lot of effort.

80. Networking should be a way of life – not something you do when you are out of work.

81.
Networking is about building and nurturing relationships.

82.

The architect of market reforms that transformed the antiquated and backward Chinese economy into what it is today was arrested.

83.

When doing business in China, remember ~ it isn't Kansas.

42 The Tao of Supply Chain Management

84.

Learn the difference between *offshoring* and *outsourcing*.

85.
There is no such thing as a perfect storm.

86. If information were power, the librarians would own the world.

87.
The real power lies in the ability to identify relevant information and act upon it.

88. If you have leverage, use it.

89.

If you don't have any, find some.

90.

Beware of using all the latest buzz words and terms to show your knowledge of the supply chain.

91.

If you know what you are talking about, your audience will know it, as well.

92.

Many still think that a value prop is the inexpensive, club-store brand of outboard motor accessory.

93.

"Best in Class" is the sixth grader who can recite "Abu Ben Adam" without a misstep.

94.

Untenable is a number that is not divisible by 10.

95.

Many good logisticians haven't mastered the skills required for effective supply chain management – human relations skills, negotiating expertise, and a knack for fostering collaboration and integration among the various functions.

96.

If they expect to succeed in the new environment, they must find a way to acquire them.

97.

Try to eliminate the term 3PL from your vocabulary.

98. Try to replace it with LSP.

99.

If you cannot do this, learn the definitions of 3PL, 4PL, and LLP.

100. Repeat them over and over until you get them right.

101. Reconsider using LSP.

102.

Technology, in and of itself, has no value.

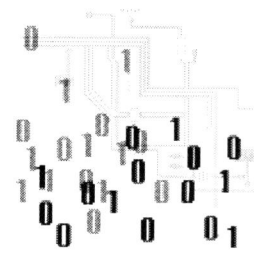

103. If you don't know what an agile supply chain is, just try to keep it flexible.

104.

Major failures in outsourcing relationships occur when a firm outsources an activity its own personnel do not totally comprehend, and the provider promises to meet requirements that have not been clearly defined, communicated or understood.

105. While technology most often is identified as the major obstacle to Collaborative Planning, Forecasting and Replenishment (CPFR), there is considerable evidence to suggest that lack of cooperation among and even *within* companies is a major factor.

106. In the final analysis, the success or failure of CPFR will be dictated, not by technology, but by human skills, attitudes and actions.

107. Keep in mind that your new best friend may be the person who never returned your telephone calls who is now out of work.

108.
The only true, total supply chain executive in a firm is the chief executive officer.

109. Not all SCM consultants are between jobs.

110. Some do it because they want to.

111.

Managing a proactive supply chain is preferred.

112.
Being reactive is not so good.

113.

The second most powerful force in SCM improvement, right behind IT, is Wal-Mart.

114. Not all motor carriers are orange.

115.

It only seems that way.

116. Do not ignore RFID.

117.

Any outsourcing relationship should be covered by a well-defined, legally-sound contract that should be executed *before* the operation starts up.

118. A good LSP will offer value-added services.

119. A good LSP is customer-focused.

120.
A good LSP is technology-driven.

121.

The best LSP's will be relationship-conscious.

122.

The supply chain manager must strike a fine balance between being a problem solver and a leader.

123.
Tony Soprano's crew has a clear mission and purpose.

124.
So should the supply chain manager's.

125.

The real value of freight bill payment services is in the business intelligence generated by the provider.

126. Foreign Trade Zone is a government-sanctioned site where foreign and domestic materials are considered by the United States Customs Service to be in international commerce.

127.
While in the zone, the materials may be stored, manipulated, mixed with domestic and/or foreign materials, used in assembly or manufacturing processes, or exhibited for sale without the payment of duty and excise taxes.

128. A good supply chain manager will understand FTZ's and their possible applications to his/her firm's supply chain.

129. The complexity of global logistics will raise the technology bar.

130.

Not all brokers are named Joe Bob and think chicken fried steak is a delicacy.

131.

The use of a freight broker will give managers the ability to gain expanded access to available motor carrier capacity.

132.

Exercise the same care in selecting a freight broker as you would in the procurement of other logistics services.

133.

Beware of LSP's that are interested only in being the low bidder.

134. Who pays well is served well.

135.

Be sure your LSP has a commitment to continuous improvement in performance and customer satisfaction.

136.

The best executive is the one who has sense enough to pick good people to do what she wants done, and self restraint enough to keep from meddling with them while they do it.

137.

An order of magnitude is a large order.

138.

Hold your friends close.

139. Hold your enemies closer.

140.
Choose your consigliere carefully.

141.

Pay him well.

142.

Develop ancient skills…

143.
…Write a real letter.

144.

An articulate, well-researched presentation is worth a thousand PowerPoints.

145. The newer container ships are 34 feet wider than the Panama Canal.

146. The rewards for a successful outsourcing relationship can be great, but the price of failure can be high.

147. If all traffic moves around a warehouse counterclockwise, drivers will never have to back in from the blind side.

148.

To a consultant, the "C-Level" is senior management.

149. To the huddled masses, it is the third floor of the parking garage.

150.

Choose your battles carefully.

151.

Even Don Quixote didn't tilt at every windmill.

152.

If you are the weakest link in the supply chain, when it breaks, you will not escape unscathed.

The Tao of Supply Chain Management 71

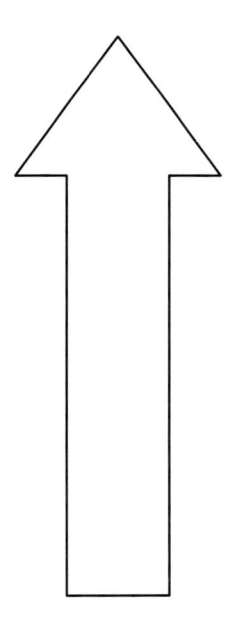

153. Manage up.

154.

The higher you rise in the organization, the more meetings you will attend.

155. The more meetings you attend, the less you will get done.

156. Avoid meetings at all costs.

157. Cross-functional teams preclude any one person having to make a decision.

158.

Doing things as they have always been done will result in the same, albeit safe, mediocre performance.

159.

Work hard, but maintain balance in your life.

160.

If you are what you do, then when you don't do it anymore, you aren't.

The Tao of Supply Chain Management

76 The Tao of Supply Chain Management

The Tao of Supply Chain Management

C. F. Lynch & Associates offers a complete menu of supply chain management advisory services. We work closely with client management to understand needs, analyze supply chain functions, and offer alternatives that reduce costs or add value and improve customer service.

We have experience and expertise in a number of areas, including
- Logistics Management
- Strategic Logistics Planning
- Industry Research
- Case Study Writing
- Management Evaluation and Recruiting
- Organization and Training
- Warehouse Administration and Operations
- Market Research and Marketing of Services
- Outsourcing Planning and Evaluation
- Third Party Analysis, Selection and Negotiation
- Distribution Center Location Analysis
- Merger and Acquisition
- Carrier Rate Negotiations and Selection
- Industrial Real Estate Brokerage

Call us to discuss how we might assist you.

C. F. Lynch & Associates
5100 Poplar Avenue, Suite 522
Memphis, TN 38137
901/415-6800
901/415-6810 Fax
E-mail: cliff@cflynch.com
www.cflynch.com